Investigate

Push and Pull

Charlotte Guillain

Heinemann Library
Chicago, Illinois

2008 Heinemann Library
a division of Capstone Global Library, LLC.
Chicago, Illinois

Customer Service 888-454-2279
Visit our website at www.heinemannraintree.com

Designed by Joanna Hinton-Malivoire Victoria Bevan, and Hart McLeod
Printed in the United States of America in North Mankato, Minnesota. 102012 006970

14 13 12
10 9 8 7 6 5 4 3 2

The Library of Congress has cataloged the first edition as follows:
Guillain, Charlotte.
  Push and pull / Charlotte Guillain.
    p. cm. -- (Investigate)
  Includes bibliographical references and index.
  ISBN 978-1-4329-1392-2 (hc) -- ISBN 978-1-4329-1408-0 (pb) 1. Force and energy--Juvenile literature. 2. Mechanics--Juvenile literature. I. Title.
  QC73.4.G85 2008
  531'.6--dc22

                              2008006810

Acknowledgments
The publishers would like to thank the following for permission to reproduce photographs: ©Alamy pp. 23 (Laurent Hamels), 25 (Real World People), 29 (Hugh Threlfall); ©Corbis pp. 10 (Hubert Stadler), 16 (David Madison), 20 (Image100), 28 (Michael DeYoung), 26, 30; ©DK Images p. 24; ©Getty pp. 8, 30 (Dylan Ellis), 9 (Hepp), 11 (Stephen St. John), 12 (Sylvain Grandadam), 13 (Paul Kennedy), 14 (Alexander Walter), 15 (Ariel Skelley); ©Getty Images p. 7 (PhotoDisc); ©Jupiter Images p. 7, ©Nasa p. 27; ©Photolibrary pp. 4 (Rubberball Productions), 5 (GARDEL Bertrand), 6 (Image100), 18 (George Kannavas), 21 (Radius Images); ©PunchStock p. 17 (Juice Images); ©Science Photo Library p. 22 (LEONARD LESSIN); ©Superstock p. 19.

Cover photograph reproduced with permission of ©Alamy (Westend61).

Contents

Some words are shown in bold, **like this**. You can find out what they mean by looking in the glossary.

Motion

Everywhere we go things are moving around us. There are cars, buses, and trucks on the road. There are people running, riding bikes, and jumping. When things move from one place to another, they are in **motion**.

Every motion is started by a **force**. Every motion is stopped by a force. A force is a push or pull that works to make something move.

Pushing and Pulling

Movement happens when something is pushed. When you kick a ball you push it forward. When you push a door it opens. When you walk, run, or jump you are pushing on the ground with your feet.

Movement also happens when something is pulled. When you pull a drawer it opens. You put on your shoes by pulling them.

Q Do you push or pull the things in these pictures?

A You move all of the things by pushing them.

Pushing and pulling make **motion** happen. These
8 **forces** can make things move, stop, speed up, slow
down, or change direction.

Things do not move without pushing and pulling.
Things will stay still if there is no force to move them.

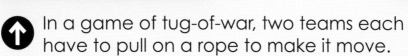 In a game of tug-of-war, two teams each
have to pull on a rope to make it move.

People can push and pull things. Air or water that
10 is moving can also push things.

Q How could you push this feather without touching it?

CLUE
- Remember: moving air can push things.

11

A If you blow at the feather, you make moving air. This will push the feather along.

Moving air, or wind, can also push sailing boats along.

The moving water in the ocean can push things on to the beach. The moving waves in the ocean move surfers through the water.

13

Speed and Distance

We push or pull things to make them move.
We can push and pull quickly or slowly.

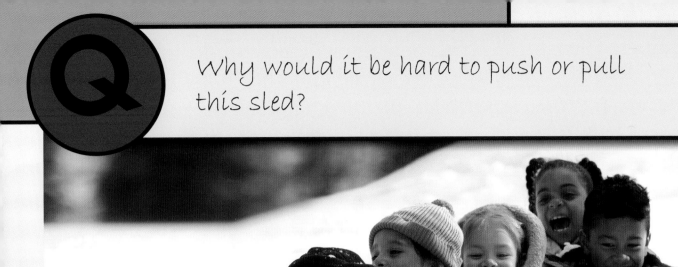

Q Why would it be hard to push or pull this sled?

CLUE
- How many children are on the sled?

A It would be hard to move the sled because it is heavy. Heavy objects need bigger pushes and pulls. It is hard to move heavy things quickly.

16

Lighter objects need smaller pushes and pulls. They are much easier to move than heavy objects. It is easier to move light things quickly.

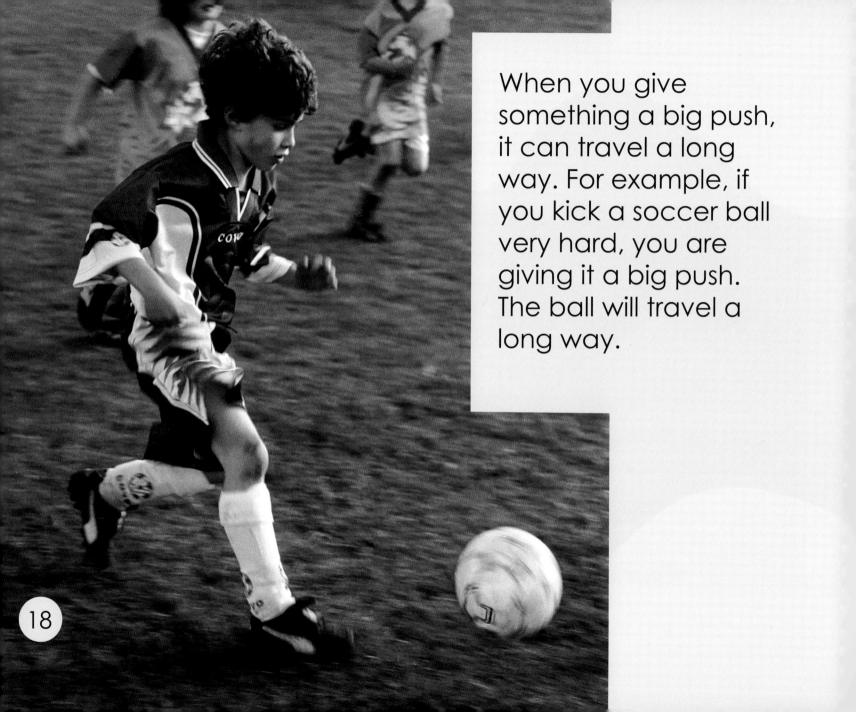

When you give something a big push, it can travel a long way. For example, if you kick a soccer ball very hard, you are giving it a big push. The ball will travel a long way.

18

When you give something a small push, it does not travel very far. For example, if you tap a golf ball into a hole, you are giving it a small push. The ball will travel a short distance.

Stopping

We also push and pull things to stop them from moving. You grab and pull on a door that is swinging shut to stop it from moving. You put out your hand to stop a toy car from moving. It is the push of your hand that stops the car.

A player's foot stops the ball by pushing it.

If we give something a big push or pull it will stop moving more quickly. It is harder work to push or pull heavy things to stop them from moving.

 Moving things can be dangerous if they are heavy, or moving quickly like this swing.

Springs

A spring is a **coil** of wire. Springs change shape when we push or pull them. We use springs in lots of different ways. There are springs in staplers and some pens. Lots of toys have springs in them.

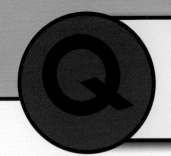

Q This spring is being pushed together. What will happen when the person lets go?

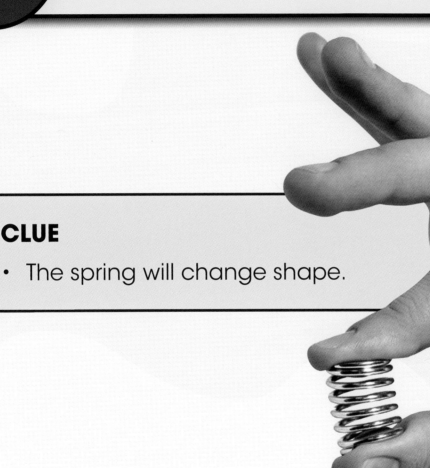

? **CLUE**

- The spring will change shape.

When the person lets go, the spring will move up.

When we push a spring down, the spring pushes back up against our hand. When we pull a spring up, the spring pulls on our hand.

24

spring

Springs help to make things move. When a spring has been pushed down it will always push back up. This **motion** can be used to move objects. Springs can be used in clocks, toys, and other machines to make them move.

25

Gravity

Gravity is the **force** that pulls everything to the center of Earth. If you drop a ball, gravity will pull it down to the ground. The pull of gravity holds us on Earth's surface. Without gravity we would float in the air above the ground.

The pull of gravity makes things move downhill.

When **astronauts** travel into outer space, they move away from the center of Earth. There is no pull of gravity in outer space. Astronauts can float around in outer space.

Forces are working around us all the time. People push and pull things every day. Pushes and pulls work to move us around. Pushes and pulls also stop us from moving.

Pushing on the pedals makes a bike move.

pedal

Wind and water also push objects into **motion**. Everything around us is being pulled by the force of gravity. Forces affect everything we do and all the movement in the world around us.

This boy is pulling himself up a climbing wall. If he lets go, the force of gravity will pull him back down to the ground.

Checklist

➡ Every **motion** is started by a **force**.

➡ Every motion is stopped by a force.

➡ A force is a push or pull that works to make something move.

➡ Heavy objects need big pushes and pulls to move.

➡ Light objects need small pushes and pulls to move.

➡ The pull of **gravity** holds us on Earth's surface.

Glossary

astronauts scientists who travel into outer space

coil something that has been wound into loops, such as a spring, or a piece of rope

force a push or a pull that makes something move

gravity the force that pulls everything down to the center of Earth

motion something moving from one place to another. When we walk we are in motion.

Index